WITHDRAWN

Introducing Habitats

A FOREST HABITAT

Bobbie Kalman

Crabtree Publishing Company

www.crabtreebooks.com

Created by Bobbie Kalman

Dedicated by Julie Alguire
For Eric and Rowan—my great outdoorsmen!

Author and Editor-in-Chief
Bobbie Kalman

Project editor
Kelley MacAulay

Editors
Molly Aloian
Michael Hodge
Kathryn Smithyman

Design
Katherine Kantor
Margaret Amy Salter (cover)
Samantha Crabtree (series logo)

Production coordinator
Heather Fitzpatrick

Photo research
Crystal Foxton

Special thanks to
Jack Pickett and Karen Van Atte

Illustrations
Barbara Bedell: pages 8, 14-15, 32 (top)
Margaret Amy Salter: pages 12, 13, 17, 32 (bottom)

Photographs
iStockphoto.com: Tim Harman: page 10; Svetlana Prikhodko:
　page 15 (top); Ben Renard-Wiart: page 31
Visuals Unlimited: Barbara Gerlach: page 20; Jack Milchanowski:
　page 22
Other images by Adobe Image Library, Brand X Pictures, Corbis,
　Corel, Creatas, Digital Stock, Digital Vision, Eyewire, and Photodisc

Library and Archives Canada Cataloguing in Publication

Kalman, Bobbie, date.
　A forest habitat / Bobbie Kalman.

(Introducing habitats)
ISBN-13: 978-0-7787-2951-8 (bound)
ISBN-13: 978-0-7787-2979-2 (pbk.)
ISBN-10: 0-7787-2951-6 (bound)
ISBN-10: 0-7787-2979-6 (pbk.)

　1. Forest ecology--Juvenile literature.　I. Title.　II. Series.

QH541.5.F6K34 2006　　j577.3　　C2006-904124-5

Library of Congress Cataloging-in-Publication Data

Kalman, Bobbie.
　A forest habitat / Bobbie Kalman.
　　p. cm. -- (Introducing habitats)
　ISBN-13: 978-0-7787-2951-8 (rlb)
　ISBN-10: 0-7787-2951-6 (rlb)
　ISBN-13: 978-0-7787-2979-2 (pb)
　ISBN-10: 0-7787-2979-6 (pb)
　1. Forest ecology--Juvenile literature.　I. Title.　II. Series.

QH541.5.F6K345 2007
577.3--dc22

2006023327

Crabtree Publishing Company

www.crabtreebooks.com　　　1-800-387-7650

Published in Canada
Crabtree Publishing
616 Welland Ave.
St. Catharines, ON
L2M 5V6

Published in the United States
Crabtree Publishing
PMB16A
350 Fifth Ave., Suite 3308
New York, NY 10118

Published in the United Kingdom
Crabtree Publishing
White Cross Mills
High Town, Lancaster
LA1 4XS

Published in Australia
Crabtree Publishing
386 Mt. Alexander Rd.
Ascot Vale (Melbourne)
VIC 3032

Contents

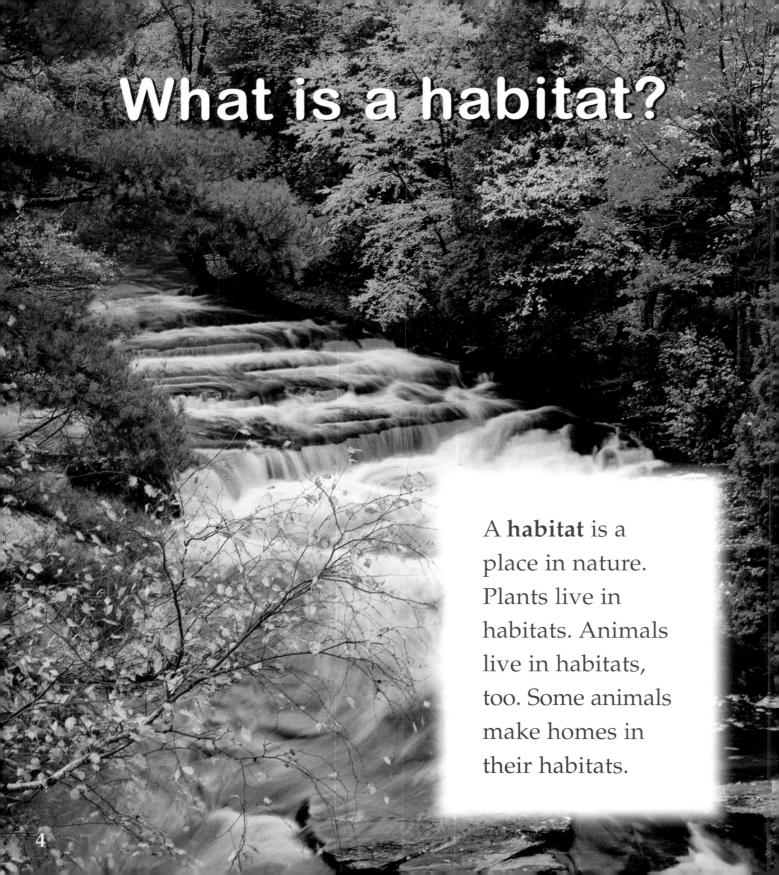

What is a habitat?

A **habitat** is a place in nature. Plants live in habitats. Animals live in habitats, too. Some animals make homes in their habitats.

Living and non-living things

There are **living things** in habitats. Plants and animals are living things. There are also **non-living things** in habitats. Rocks, water, and dirt are non-living things.

living thing

non-living thing

Everything they need

Plants and animals need air,
water, and food to stay alive.
Everything plants and animals
need is in their habitats. This
squirrel found food in its habitat.

At home in their habitats

Some animals have homes in their habitats. These baby foxes have a home. Their home is under a dead tree. The baby foxes live under the tree.

Forest habitats

Forests are habitats. Forests are places where many trees grow. Many other plants also grow in forests. Mosses and bushes grow in forests.

moss on a rock

Four seasons

Some forests are in parts of the world that are always hot. Other forests are in parts of the world that are always cold. This book is about forests that are in parts of the world with four **seasons**. The seasons are spring, summer, autumn, and winter. This porcupine is in a forest in spring.

Forest weather

The weather in forest habitats changes as the seasons change. Spring is warm and rainy. Warm, rainy weather helps trees grow in forests. Summer weather is hot. This baby opossum is walking through a forest in summer.

Colder weather

In autumn, the weather is cool. On autumn mornings, **frost** often forms on forest plants. Frost is a thin layer of ice. In winter, the weather is cold. Snow covers the ground and the trees in forests. This baby cougar is in a forest in winter.

11

Two types of trees

Forests that are in parts of the world with four seasons have two types of trees. One type of tree has wide, flat leaves. These leaves turn orange, red, or yellow in autumn. Then they fall from the trees.

In spring, wide, flat leaves grow on some trees. Other trees have needle-shaped leaves.

In summer, wide, flat leaves are green. Needle-shaped leaves are also green in summer.

Needle-leaves

The other type of tree has needle-shaped leaves. Needle-shaped leaves do not change color. They do not fall off trees in autumn. The trees keep their green needles in every season.

In autumn, wide, flat leaves change color. They fall from trees. Needle-shaped leaves do not change color or fall from trees.

In winter, some trees have no leaves. Their wide, flat leaves are gone. Trees with needle-shaped leaves still have their leaves.

13

The forest floor

Many plants grow on the ground in forests. In a forest, the ground is called the **forest floor**. Bushes, grasses, and other plants grow on the forest floor. Many animals eat these plants.

A lot of life

Many small animals live on the forest floor. Earthworms and beetles dig through the soil. Ants crawl across the forest floor. Millipedes live under dead trees and dead leaves. They eat the dead leaves.

ants

millipede

15

Plants make food

Living things need food. Plants make their own food. They use sunlight, air, and water to make food. Making food from sunlight, air, and water is called **photosynthesis**.

Parts for making food

A plant gets sunlight through its leaves. It also gets air through its leaves. The plant gets water through its roots. The plant uses sunlight, air, and water to make food.

Leaves take in sunlight.

Leaves take in air.

Roots take in water from the soil.

17

Forest animals

Many animals live in forest habitats. The animals on these pages live in forest habitats. Their bodies are suited to their forest habitats.

A deer eats twigs off trees. A deer's long legs and neck help it reach twigs high up on trees.

A woodpecker uses its sharp beak to find insects in tree trunks.

A butterfly flies around a forest drinking sweet liquids from flowers.

A skunk uses its long claws to dig up food from the forest floor.

A lynx uses its sharp claws to climb trees.

A chipmunk eats the seeds of trees. It stuffs the seeds into its cheeks to carry the food to its home.

19

Tree houses

Many forest animals make homes in trees. Their homes are high above the ground. Raccoons, squirrels, and birds make homes in trees. Bird homes are called **nests**. Baby birds are born in nests. This robin is in her nest with her babies.

Trees on the ground

When trees die, they fall to the ground. Some animals make homes in dead trees. This baby bobcat's home is in a dead tree.

21

On the forest floor

Some animals live on the forest floor. Copperhead snakes make homes called **dens** on the forest floor. Their dens are holes in the ground. Copperhead snakes often share their dens with other snakes.

Wanderers

Some animals do not make homes.
They wander from place to place.
The animals wander looking for
food. Moose wander in forests.

In the water

There are **streams** running through some forests. Streams have shallow, moving water. Some animals live by forest streams. Minks live by forest streams. Many minks dig homes in the mud that is on the edges of streams.

Visiting forest streams

Many animals visit forest streams. Birds and other animals bathe in the water. The animals also drink the water. Bears and other animals catch fish from the water. They eat the fish.

Forest food

Animals find food in their habitats. Many forest animals are **herbivores**. Herbivores are animals that eat only plants. Snails are herbivores. They eat leaves and moss.

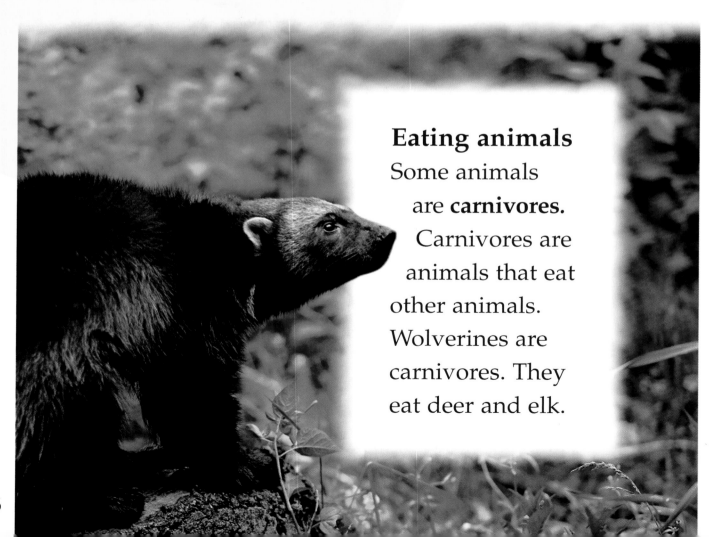

Eating animals
Some animals are **carnivores**. Carnivores are animals that eat other animals. Wolverines are carnivores. They eat deer and elk.

Eating anything

Some animals are **omnivores**.
Omnivores eat both plants and animals.
Wild turkeys are omnivores. They eat
acorns, seeds, and leaves. They also
eat insects, spiders, and salamanders.

Getting energy

sun

All living things need **energy**. Energy helps living things grow and move. Energy comes from the sun. Plants use the sun's energy to make food. Animals get energy by eating. A woodrat is a herbivore. It gets energy by eating leaves.

leaves

woodrat

Energy for carnivores

A carnivore gets energy by eating other animals. A spotted owl is a carnivore. It gets energy by eating a woodrat.

Warm in winter

In autumn, many forest animals grow thicker fur. The thick fur keeps the animals warm in cold, winter weather. This wolf has thick winter fur.

Moving on

Winter weather is too cold for some animals. These animals leave their forest habitats in autumn. They travel to warmer habitats for the winter. In spring, they return to their habitats. The weather becomes warm again in spring. Red-shouldered hawks fly to warm habitats for winter.

Words to know and Index

animals
pages 4, 5, 6, 7, 14, 15, 18-19, 20, 21, 22, 23, 24, 25, 26, 27, 28, 29, 30, 31

energy
pages 28-29

food
pages 6, 16, 17, 19, 23, 26-27, 28

forests
pages 8, 9, 10, 11, 12, 14, 15, 18, 20, 22, 23, 24, 25, 26, 30, 31

habitats
pages 4, 5, 6, 7, 8, 10, 18, 26, 31

homes
pages 4, 7, 19, 20-23, 24

plants
pages 4, 5, 6, 8, 11, 14, 16, 17, 26, 27, 28

trees
pages 7, 8, 10, 11, 12-13, 15, 19, 20, 21

Other index words

Printed in the U.S.A.